MAR 2001

ART

"Most of the beauty in San Diego is yet to
come," we said in 1962.

May this book help you to create beauty in
the city in your own way, and according to
the best ideas of your era. Please make a
wide search for good design ideas.

Best wishes for a handsome community in
the next century.

L Ruocco AIA
Ilse Hamann Ruocco

Presented to the San Diego Public Library by the
Lloyd and Ilse Ruocco Fund, a part of The San
Diego Foundation

September, 2000

San Diego Public Library

SLEEPING SPACES

SLEEPING SPACES

DESIGNS FOR REST AND RENEWAL   LISA SKOLNIK

3 1336 05359 1922

Copyright © 2000 by Rockport Publishers, Inc.

All rights reserved. No part of this book may be reproduced in any form without written per-
mission of the copyright owners. All images in this book have been reproduced with the knowl-
edge and prior consent of the artists concerned and no responsibility is accepted by producer,
publisher, or printer for any infringement of copyright or otherwise, arising from the contents
of this publication. Every effort has been made to ensure that credits accurately comply with
information supplied.

First published in the United States of America by
Rockport Publishers, Inc.
33 Commercial Street
Gloucester, Massachusetts 01930-5089
Telephone: (978) 282-9590
Facsimile: (978) 283-2742

ISBN 1-56496-622-4

10 9 8 7 6 5 4 3 2 1

Design: Leeann Leftwich
Cover image by Peter Margonelli, design by Benjamin Noriega-Ortiz.

Printed in China.

The Bed

12

Pure Sleep

38

Havens for Relaxation

64

Contents

Introduction   8

Siestas

90

Bedroom Retreats

120

Afterword   156

Directory of Designers
and Photographers   158

Introduction

THERE ARE FEW CERTAINTIES IN LIFE, BUT ONE OF THEM IS THE NEED TO SLEEP. IT'S SOMETHING ALL OF US DO—REGARDLESS OF WHO WE ARE, WHERE WE RESIDE, AND HOW WE LIVE—SINCE IT'S CRITICAL TO OUR PHYSICAL AND EMOTIONAL WELL-BEING. AND IT'S SOMETHING WE SPEND A CONSIDERABLE AMOUNT OF TIME DOING; THE AVERAGE EIGHT HOURS A NIGHT AMOUNTS TO A THIRD OF OUR LIVES, AND THAT DOESN'T ACCOUNT FOR OUR MOMENTS SPENT IN REPOSE.

Not surprisingly, restoring ourselves calls for more than sleep alone. Every home needs a sanctuary where one can escape from the hustle and bustle of everyday life, or a secluded spot to just relax and revitalize. Ideally, these spaces should nurture our tired bodies and sustain our weary souls. They must cocoon us in comfort, but if they also happen to seduce us with the promise of serenity and inner peace, or perhaps manage to transport us away from the issues of everyday life, all the better. It's not hard to imagine the sort of space that will do this or to realize that creating them takes planning, imagination, resourcefulness, and, most likely, work.

At the very least, just about every home has at least one bedroom, but most of us have several spaces we use for sleep. We may have several bedrooms, and there are also the spots we use for routine naps or the occasional stolen snooze. An extra-plump sofa in the family room, a cozy chair in the study, the pliant chaise in the sunroom, or even right outside all qualify, and as such need to be designed to accommodate these activities. Yet sleeping spaces, be it our bedrooms or the nooks and crannies we use for resting, have traditionally been the last parts of our homes to receive the kind of attention we grant to our homes' public spaces, which we perceive as more important. The bedroom is usually the last space to be decorated, renovated, or upgraded, and the least attention is given its maintenance. And those spaces we use for our snoozes are a matter of happenstance rather than planning.

Today, research supports the notion that a bedroom, or any other space that accommodates sleep and its related activities, should be more than just a randomly arrayed place to sleep. It must fulfill a variety of physical, psychological, and emotional needs. Our bodies have certain requirements in repose that must be met, and these relate to the structural composition of the furnishings we use and the environment that surrounds us. There are very specific parameters that should be met in a space to ensure restful and restorative slumber.

Given all these issues, it is clear that our sleeping spaces should embrace, incorporate, and even reconcile numerous elements. They must be functional, comfortable, nurturing, appealing to the eye, and, above all else, restful and serene. There are also myriad concerns to address when creating them, such as the architecture, furnishings, lighting, soundproofing, and the use of color. Furthermore, many of these concerns are in flux, for advancements in technology and achievements in design are constantly effecting changes in the performance and appearance of these elements.

On the following pages is a series of well-designed and effective environments that are devoted to, or used in part for, sleep. They are attractive, comfortable, restful, serene, nurturing, and, most importantly, supremely functional, since they encourage or inspire sleep. No matter what the decorating style, promoting this activity came first in planning, executing, and decorating these successful environments. The results are spaces that are can be used for guidance in creating your own sleeping spaces.

DESIGN CAROL THOMAS / PHOTO SIMON UPTON

the bed

THE BED PRESIDES OVER THE ROOM IT INHABITS, AND FOR GOOD REASON. IT SHOULDERS A SIGNIFICANT FUNCTION AND BEARS A SIZABLE FORM.

These realities make its appearance and placement critical in the design and effectiveness of the bedroom. Fortunately, it doesn't take much to let the bed set the tone or organize the floor plan for an entire space.

For instance, a plank bed frame elicits a rustic or provincial aura; one in polished metal or glossed wood may impart a modern or minimal aesthetic. Bedclothes are just as evocative. Frothy linens turn a bed sweet and romantic; crisp textiles lend it an air of tailored elegance; and rich trappings give a bed a lavish, or even extravagant, demeanor. Place a bed smack in the center of the room for a very different impact than one that is up against a wall or secluded in a corner.

Thanks to its powerful presence, changing the bed can also change the very nature of the room. And making those changes can be as easy and inexpensive as dressing and draping the bed to evoke a new mood or enhance its allure. Drenching it with color and pattern can offer definition by establishing a specific decorative style or increasing the contrast with the rest of its surroundings. These devices also set the bed apart from plain walls and floors, or the reverse; subtle patterns and hues become an oasis in a sea of pattern. Tenting the bed in various ways establishes a certain tone, be it historic, exotic, fanciful, or romantic.

To endow the bedroom with a serene and nurturing aura, opt for simplicity. A bed can tempt and entice without all the fussy attire. Elegance and ease meet head-on here, thanks to deftly chosen elements that speak to function and form such as a minimally dressed ,but beckoning bed cool bandlue-green cabinetry hat lends the space a soothing demeanor.

PHOTO ANTOINE BOOTZ

And changing the look of your bed need not be a big production. For example, you can create the look of a canopy bed without building a new structure. Simply hang fabric from a central point over the head of the bed. Then, drape lengths of lightweight cotton over hooks in the ceiling placed at either side of the head of the bed for a contemporary effect or at all four corners for a very dramatic effect.

Whatever types of textiles are employed, it is important to consider the cleaning process. Sheets, pillowcases, quilt covers, and shams need frequent laundering, so they should be able to withstand regular washings. They must be colorfast, shrink-resistant, and require little, or preferably no, special care such as hand washing or air-drying. It is best to use products that are designed for this purpose instead of bed linens made of unusual fabrics. However, dust ruffles, valences, and tents do not need to be washed as frequently and can be made of a heavier or more care-intensive cloth.

To draw attention to a simple bed, a colorful quilt and textured linens make a good start. But painting the wall a soft hue—in this case, a pale sea green that is present in the quilt—and topping the headboard with a narrow ledge that emphasizes it will increase the stature of the bed and make the bed a focal point of the room.

PHOTO COURTESY OF POTTERY BARN

Changing linens is not the only way to give your bedroom a quick makeover. introduce a unique bed such as one constructed of industrial components (metal scaffolding tubes or the metal shelving systems available at housewares stores can be used for this) or an old hospital bed or four-poster bed stripped bare of embellishments. it will change the whole look of your room.

These are just some of the elements to keep in mind when picking a bed and components that adorn it. Your most significant consideration should always be your own personal preference. Every aspect of the bed, from its comfort quotient to the style with which it is arrayed, ultimately depends on your wants, personal style, and needs.

SLEEP SECRETS

FENG SHUI DICTATES THAT THE BED SHOULD FACE THE ENTRANCE TO THE ROOM, BUT YOUR FEET SHOULD NOT BE POINTED DIRECTLY TOWARD THE DOOR SINCE THAT IS THE POSITION ASSOCIATED WITH DEATH (YOUR BODY IS CARRIED FROM THE ROOM IN THIS POSITION). THE BED SHOULD ALSO HAVE ITS HEAD AGAINST A WALL TO ENSURE SOLIDITY, STABILITY, AND SECURITY, AND IF A COUPLE SHARES THE BED, THERE SHOULD BE AN EQUAL AMOUNT OF SPACE ON BOTH SIDES OF THE BED.

For a romantic look minus the frills, opt for a contemporary canopy bed with clean lines. This version is made of metal and dressed with close-fitting linens that are inviting yet streamlined. Button-trimmed shams (you can also use embroidered shams) and a vivid paisley throw add decorative details that are tailored but sumptuous at the same time.

DESIGN JULA SUTTA / PHOTO COLIN MCRAE

A bed has carte blanche to take center stage in an architecturally arresting room, but the trick to carrying it off is restraint. All that is needed in a room with bones like this one is an equally spare bedspread with only a touch of texture.

PHOTO ERIC ROTH

headboard **solutions**

WHILE LINENS ARE PERHAPS THE EASIEST WAYS TO IMPLEMENT A QUICK CHANGE IN THE BEDROOM, DON'T FORGET THE HEADBOARD. A MAKESHIFT HEADBOARD IS EASY TO DECORATE AND SIMPLE TO INSTALL, AND CAN TOTALLY REVAMP THE IMAGE OF A BED. FIND AN OLD ONE WITHOUT RUNNERS OR A FOOTBOARD AND EMBELLISH IT WITH AN EASY CRAFT TECHNIQUE (SOME DECORATIVE OPTIONS INCLUDE DECOUPAGE, STENCILING, PAPERING, FAUX FINISHING, OR MOSAICS MADE OF TILES, BUTTONS, OR BEADS). WHEN FINISHED, WEDGE YOUR NEW HEADBOARD BETWEEN THE BED AND A WALL TO STABILIZE IT.

- Fence yourself in. Take picket or slat fencing and cut it to measure, matching the width of the bed. Or wrap it around the edges to snugly enclose the head of the bed. Leave it in its natural state for a rugged or primitive look, or embellish it with stain or paint for something more refined. You can even opt for a fretwork fence painted white to evoke a Victorian aura.

- Crown the head. Instead of creating a tented treatment with a bed crown and fabric, use an arbor. Buy one ready-made at a garden store, or make one out of lattice panels. In either case, you can also cut a piece of plywood to match the shape of the arbor, cover it with batting and fabric in a garden or floral pattern with a staple gun, and nail it to the back of the arbor to head the bed.

- Take plain plywood and have it cut in any shape desired. Upholster it with batting and sheeting using a staple gun. Or embellish it with tiles, shells, buttons, or even large glass beads in an attractive or dramatic pattern. A variety of glues is available that will allow these objects to be permanently attached to the wood.

- A textile can be draped or hung on the wall behind the bed to take the place of a headboard. Best of all, it can be installed in a range of easy decorative options. Tack a quilt on the wall right behind the bed. Or take a simple curtain rod and nail it to the wall, then cover it with a length of fabric twice or three times as long as the rod for a shirred effect. For a rustic approach, tie fabric to a long branch that functions as a pole, or use a box-pleated sheet and tack it to the wall at the pleats.

FAR RIGHT Crisp, perfectly unblemished linens, properly fluffed and perfectly arrayed, make a bed inviting. A subtle tone-on-tone play of beige, white, and icy blue hues enhances the well-groomed aura of the bed and lends it a touch of warmth.

PHOTO TIM STREET-PORTER

RIGHT Opulence doesn't have to be exorbitantly expensive. Bargain textiles from a variety of sources can be layered on a bed and surrounded with equally inexpensive furnishings that have the right amount of glitz. A piece of wood embellished with plaster medallions and covered with metallic paint makes a resplendent headboard.

PHOTO TONY BERARDI

BELOW Sometimes it pays to play against type. Posh Ultrasuede on this low platform bed enhances the spare tatami mats and shoji screens that outfit the rest of the room, yet still jibe with the simplicity of the setting.

DESIGN TANGEE HARRIS-PRICHETT /
PHOTO DOROTHY PERRY

OPPOSITE Color and pattern, no matter how subtle, boost the perceived comfort quotient and cachet of a bed. Creamy tones of maize spiked with touches of green make this simple iron bed alluring. Using these soft, warm tones gives this room a sense of identity that sets it apart from the cool, blue-toned bedroom across the hall.

PHOTO ERIC ROTH

ABOVE Enough beds to accommodate guests are a luxury if space is at a premium. The concept of a true dormitory is revisited and refined in this guest room, where the streamlined beds are actually berths that emulate a stateroom on an ocean liner. Drawers for storage are below the bottom berths.

DESIGN LONN FRYE/ PHOTO TONY BERARDI

OPPOSITE When wall space is at a premium, get creative. A window makes a suitable backdrop for a bed, especially if the window has some design cachet of its own, as in the case of this small country room with its simple iron bed. If nature is your backdrop, emphasize it with bright, sunny bedclothes.

PHOTO COURTESY OF POTTERY BARN

SLEEP SECRETS

A BED THAT FACES THE DOOR CAN GIVE ITS OCCUPANTS A SENSE OF SECURITY WHEN THEY ARE MOST VULNERABLE, SINCE THEY CAN EASILY SEE WHO IS ENTERING THE ROOM. IT IS ALSO PRACTI-CAL TO POSITION A BED AGAINST A WALL IN SUCH A WAY THAT THERE IS PLENTY OF SPACE AROUND IT. THIS OFTEN MAKES THE MOST OPTIMAL USE OF SQUARE FOOTAGE, SINCE IT SITUATES THE BED AT ONE END OF THE ROOM AND ALLOWS EASY ACCESS TO ALL ITS SIDES FOR ITS OCCUPANTS AND WHOEVER MAKES AND CHANGES IT.

ABOVE This bedroom proves that simple is indeed elegant. And what could be simpler than using plain white sheets to adorn a bed? Add small black pillows (or a dark color such as navy blue) for contrast and you'll go from stark to stylish for a decidedly elegant decor. Tacked to the wall behind the bed and trimmed with tassels, they become a sophisticated stand-in for a headboard and suggest a canopy.

PHOTO TONY BERARDI

LEFT A bed that has a significant amount of architectural cachet of its own is best dressed simply to let the good lines show. Plain white trappings emphasize its form and keep it from acquiring flamboyant airs.

PHOTO COURTESY OF THE MORSON COLLECTION

ABOVE To create a formal look for your bed, improvise. Use a subtly textured cover, instead of a bedspread, which envelopes the mattress using simple, folded corners. Crisp linens with sharply contrasting hues create a clean, tailored look.

PHOTO COURTESY OF SPIEGEL

OPPOSITE Add built-in shelves around the bed to suggest a headboard where there is none while at the same time providing great open storage and, in this case, offering an arresting framework for a dramatic work of art. By painting the shelves black, their decorative prowess increased, as they seem to cocoon the bed.

PHOTO TONY BERARDI

maximizing **your mattress**

THE AVERAGE LIFE OF MOST MATTRESSES
IS ABOUT TEN YEARS. BUT THE QUALITY OF
THE MATTRESS AND THE KIND OF USE IT
RECEIVES ALSO MATTER. DETERIORATION
INSIDE A MATTRESS CAN OFTEN GO
UNNOTICED UNTIL YOUR BODY STARTS
FEELING IT. THE STIFFNESS AND PAIN
FROM TOSSING AND TURNING ARE GOOD
INDICATORS OF AN OLD MATTRESS. IT IS
STILL CRITICAL TO GIVE YOUR SLEEP SET
A THOROUGH GOING-OVER TWICE A
YEAR, TO CHECK FOR PEAKS, VALLEYS,
LUMPS, BUMPS, AND SURFACE WEAR
AND TEAR.

SELECTING A NEW MATTRESS

Follow these tips to select a new mattress that will provide years of sound sleeping:

1 Lie down on the job. Try out the mattress before buying it, paying attention to its give, feel, and firmness.

2 Pick a size that fits. Sleepers shift positions between forty and sixty times a night, so the bigger the bed the less chance you have of disturbing your partner. A full-size bed is 53 inches (135 cm) wide and offers a couple the same amount of space that a crib offers a baby. Mattresses are also getting thicker—you can find some that are 15 inches (38 cm) thick. These aren't necessarily better; they just provide a different feel.

3 Keep it firm. There is no scientific data on what type is best, but experts agree that a mattress should offer adequate, comfortable, consistent support. Find the firmest one and go down a notch from there.

4 Be foundation savvy. Foundations are usually box springs, but they can also be wood platforms with slats, solid boards, or a wooden or metal frame with heavy-gauge springs. Wooden frames can make a mattress seem harder than it is and are adequate only if the wood is straight and free of cracks. All foundations are engineered to go with the mattresses they hold; substitutions are not recommended and most warranties only cover sets (the foundation and mattress) sold together. Mismatching sets or adding boards between the pieces can reduce the comfort and life span of the product.

5 Buy new. A mattress made with all-new materials is better, offering more support and durability.

KEEPING YOUR MATTRESS IN SHAPE

Just like a good sofa, a mattress needs attention and care to keep it in good shape. To keep a mattress fit:

1. Turn and rotate a brand-new mattress every few weeks to help smooth out contours. After a few months, rotate it twice a year to equalize the wear and tear it receives. A good way to keep track of timing is to complete the process when the clocks are changed. Or try the first day of spring and the first day of autumn—anything that will help mark the twice yearly requirement.

2. When rotating the mattress, don't rely on the handles to support its full weight. They are usually designed to help position the mattress over the foundation, and may pull out and damage the fabric if used improperly.

3. Check the mattress for wear and tear when rotating it. Take stock and keep track of any worn spots on the ticking or any lumps, peaks, and valleys.

4. Vacuum a mattress to keep it clean whenever it is rotated. If it's stained, stick to mild soap with a bit of cold water and rub lightly. Don't ever soak any part of the set in water.

ABOVE A trundle bed is a great way to increase play space in a children's room, and if dressed astutely—as in this space, with its blue and yellow plaid sheets that match the charming country decor-it can have two distinct identities and keep two competitive siblings satisfied.

PHOTO COURTESY OF POTTERY BARN

OPPOSITE It always pays off to draw attention to the bed by emphasizing it with attractive linens, especially when you can tie a room together by doing so. Curtains that match the colors of the bed linens will make the window an appealing "headboard" when the curtains are closed at night.

PHOTO COURTESY OF POTTERY BARN

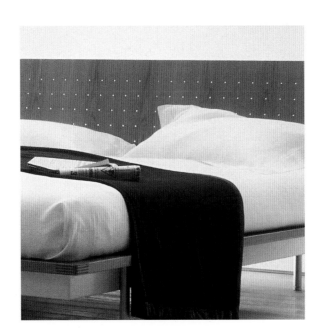

pure sleep

ALMOST A THIRD OF OUR LIFE IS SPENT SLEEPING, WHICH MAKES THE BEDROOM OUR MOST PATRONIZED—AND PRECIOUS—ROOM.

After all, it is the private sanctuary where we stretch out and relax, snatch naps, get a whole night's rest, and experience many of our most intimate moments.

Ultimately, these activities add up to much more than just a third of our lives. So why is it that despite its obvious importance, our bedroom is last on our lists when it comes to planning the decor? Perhaps this is due to the fact that it is the most private and secluded room of all. We are the only ones to actually use it, and do so most often when we are asleep and oblivious to our surroundings. So even though no one else-save members of our immediate family-might actually see this room, why should we bother making it look great?

To be fair, looks aren't everything, nor are they even the most critical part of the equation in this instance. We all need our bedrooms to be hardworking spaces that meet a range of wants and needs. The bedroom must be comforting enough to lull us to sleep, cozy enough to serve as a retreat, or able to accommodate prosaic extras such as offering up a secluded spot to read or a cozy spot to watch television.

On top of all this, the bedroom must be extremely serviceable since it usually must harbor some of our most treasured possessions and contain all of our accessories and clothes. And there is also much to do in this space on a daily basis, such as grooming ourselves, selecting our clothes, and getting dressed. If we share

Play to the strengths of a space. If the fenestration in a room is interesting, such as this huge translucent floor-to-ceiling window, keep it bare to impart the merits of its design to the rest of the room. If a space is oddly shaped, search out just the right piece of furniture to fit into its confines, such as this narrow armoire that just fits under a slanted ceiling.

PHOTO TIM STREET-PORTER

the bedroom with a partner, the room must accommodate twice as many effects and double the action. Thanks to these demands, it is important that a bedroom incorporate sufficient storage space and be configured for efficiency. Regardless of all the necessities we need to eke out of this room, getting a good night's sleep should be its paramount purpose. Thus, it is just as important to plan a bedroom as it is to plan any other space in a home. And because this is a relatively private room were we can indulge ourselves, cater to our preferences, or even let our imaginations run wild, it is all the more fun to design and decorate.

But before we can enjoy the design process, we must consider the essentials. Make sure you have a comfortable bed that fits your needs as well as restful surroundings that allow you to use the room for its most important purpose-getting a good night's sleep. Much of this depends on how you organize, outfit, and illuminate the room.

A sense of separation from other activities in the home is critical for a bedroom. Achieving this will involve where you place the bed and how you dress it. If a bedroom has too much going on in the space, it can be helpful to isolate the bed in one part of the room, or isolate it with fabric treatments that range from half-canopies and crowns to full-scale drapes layered over the rods of a four-poster bed.

Light and sound control are also critical issues. If there are many windows in the room, hang thick curtains or blinds to block outside lights. On the other hand, morning light is a powerful wake-up tool, so window treatments that are flexible enough to be adjusted to either filter or block the light are ideal. If the room is noisy, introduce plush carpets, thick drapes, or wall hangings to muffle extraneous or loud sounds.

Since this bedroom is a bit small for this imposing bed, several decorative devices have been used to expand the space. The most obvious is color, with a dusty sage green imbuing the walls with a rich intensity that gives the space more depth, but an unobtrusive collection of picture frames on a ledge above the bed draws the eye up and adds height to a relatively low ceiling.

DESIGN PETER WHEELER / PHOTO ERIC ROTH

Finally, make sure you have storage that is sensibly organized and sufficient enough to accommodate all your necessities. Since sleep should be paramount in this space, it makes sense to have as much under wraps and out of the way as possible. But it doesn't pay to cram everything in cabinets or closets. Plan for enough storage to properly house and organize your wardrobe for easy access on frantic mornings.

After realizing the essentials, there are many other components that can be employed to enhance the bedroom. For instance, color, pattern, and texture can be used to create a range of effects or establish a mood. And furnishings can evoke or develop specific decorative styles that change the very nature of the space. These tools are readily available to all of us and can be used easily, effectively, and economically to make our bedrooms the nurturing and engaging spaces we deserve.

SLEEP SECRETS

FOR SOME, THE SLIGHTEST LITTLE SOUND CAN WAKE YOU OUT OF A PEACEFUL SLEEP. WHILE SOME DECORATIVE DEVICES CAN ACT AS NOISE-BUSTERS, SUCH AS THICK DRAPES AND HEAVY CARPETS, THEY MAY NOT BE ENOUGH. THE NOISE-SENSITIVE MAY HAVE TO RELY ON ONE OF THE SPECIAL DEVICES ON THE MARKET THAT GENERATE SOOTHING BACK-GROUND NOISES (SOME EVEN OPT FOR A SIMPLE ELECTRIC FAN) OR ON EARPLUGS.

To give a room instant depth and intimacy, paint it a rich, dark color. Thanks to this tactic, this bright room with large picture windows acquired a suave, lairlike demeanor. The magazines and books strewn around the chair also contribute to the room's atmosphere, since they evoke the imagery of a cozy reading room.

DESIGN RAYMOND JOSEPH / PHOTO TONY BERARDI

the power of **sleep**

WE OFTEN COMPLAIN ABOUT HOW TIRED WE ARE, AND FOR GOOD REASON. STUDIES SHOW THE AVERAGE AMOUNT OF TIME WE SLEEP AT NIGHT HAS DECLINED ABOUT TWENTY PERCENT OVER THE LAST CENTURY. A RECENT STUDY BY THE NATIONAL SLEEP FOUNDATION FOUND THAT ONE-THIRD OF AMERICAN ADULTS SLEEP SIX HOURS OR LESS A NIGHT.

SLEEP DEPRIVATION CAN HAVE DIRE CONSEQUENCES. IT CAN IMPEDE EFFICIENCY, CAUSE TRAFFIC ACCIDENTS, AND INCREASE IRRITABILITY, TAKING A HUGE TOLL IN PERSONAL AND PROFESSIONAL RELATIONSHIPS. IN FACT, HEALTH STATISTICS SHOW THAT PEOPLE WHO SLEEP SIX HOURS OR LESS ARE TWICE AS LIKELY TO SUFFER ILLNESS AND PREMATURE DEATH THAN THOSE WHO SLEEP BETWEEN SIX AND TEN HOURS A NIGHT.

NO SNOOZE, YOU LOSE

The amount of rest each person needs varies, averaging seven and a half hours a night. Very few need more or less. Regardless of an individual's needs, lost sleep has a cumulative effect and should be made up immediately. Fortunately, experts say only a third of lost sleep needs to be made up to feel refreshed, and this can be done best by going to bed earlier the next night. A short nap during the day can also work. Sleeping late on weekends can wreak havoc with your regular patterns by delaying your body clock. Maintaining a regular sleep schedule is one of the best things you can do to feel refreshed on a regular basis.

Everyone occasionally wakes up in a sluggish state, called *sleep-drunkenness*. Those who suffer from this feel dazed and confused when they wake up, can sleep through alarms, or are groggy for more than fifteen minutes after waking. About 5 to 10 percent of us are prone to this condition on a constant basis, and a variety of things can trigger it for the normal person—interrupted sleep, lack of sleep, or stress. Again, a regular schedule will eliminate this problem.

SLEEP CYCLES

Keeping a regular sleep schedule will leave one well rested, with increased efficiency and improved health. During the night we alternate between two types of sleep: slow-wave, where brain activity slows and dreaming stops; and REM, where our eyes move rapidly and dreaming occurs. Slow-wave sleep is very deep, while REM sleep is lighter and its cycles last longer as the night wears on. Studies show that the body does its most intensive repair work during slow-wave sleep, and it is critical in keeping our bodies healthy and feeling refreshed.

Sleep cycles have a tremendous impact on how we feel and function on a daily basis. Even if we get a full night's sleep, if we don't get enough deep sleep we can feel irritable and tired. And research shows that as we age, we get less deep sleep. Also, it is best to wake up from REM sleep (interrupted slow-wave sleep will leave you groggy), and the longer you sleep the more likely that will occur. Going to bed earlier increases the chances even further.

KEEP IT SEPARATE

To ensure a good night's sleep, experts believe the most important consideration is to design your bedroom around sleep. It must be the most important purpose of the room. Don't relax or watch television in bed; this can become a habit and cause you to stay awake. The same is true of eating, reading, and talking on the phone. If you need to run a home office or have an exercise space in the room, try to separate the areas with curtains or some other decorative device. These activities are incompatible with sleep and can remind you of the stresses of your daily life, leading to insomnia.

RIGHT A variety of space-saving tricks can make a bedroom seem expansive instead of small. Here, a high bed topped with style-enhancing mosquito netting elevates the ceiling, and leaves plenty of room underneath the bed for pretty storage baskets that eliminate the need for a bed skirt. A table and a chair at the foot of the bed, appointed as a reading area, mine every available bit of floor space.

PHOTO COURTESY OF POTTERY BARN

BELOW Employ decorative treatments that play to the nature of a space. Though architecturally interesting, this room is also spare and calls for equally restrained trappings, such as smooth, pure, white bed linens. A single, sculptural floral arrangement provides all the color and contrast that is necessary to complement the setting.

DESIGN CHARLES STEWART / PHOTO COLIN MCRAE

ABOVE There's more to dress in your bedroom than your bed. Drape the same sheeting used on your bed behind it to give the bedroom a whole new demeanor. To change the look of the room, simply change the color of your bedsheets and backdrop.

DESIGN BENJAMIN NORIEGA-ORTIZ / PHOTO PETER MARGONELLI

LEFT One simple ingredient can change the entire nature of the bedroom when the largest element, namely the bed, is involved. Bring life and verve to neutral surroundings with a vibrant vintage quilt. Conversely, a creamy linen duvet would make the setting soothing and romantic.

PHOTO TONY BERARDI

LEFT Sometimes a platform bed will be lower to the ground than another style of bed, and in some instances, this can be a distinct advantage. The bed can fit under a short wall-to-wall window ledge, as in this room, and keep the window and its views unobstructed.

PHOTO COURTESY OF THE MORSON COLLECTION

RIGHT Screen-style windows and austere furnishings add an East-meets-West ambience to this bedroom. Framed translucent panels behind the bed and adjustable blinds allow daylight to stream into the room, which makes it easy to start the day. The ingenious platform bed also incorporates its own nightstands and built-in storage.

DESIGN TRICIA MILLER / PHOTO DAVID GLOMB

BELOW LEFT Call attention to the bed by hanging a series of identically framed photographs over the headboard, which, in the case of this bedroom, also broadens the bed's contours to luxurious proportions, while vertically striped linens add length. A tufted frame provides a lavish finishing touch.

DESIGN SHELLY HANDMAN / PHOTO TONY BERARDI

A balanced composition can unify a wide range of furnishings and keep them from overwhelming a room. Considered alone, these elements are relatively disparate, yet they have been forged into a symmetrical tableau that is creative and engaging. Painting the floor a cloudy blue helped matters by emphasizing the calming blues in the milieu.

DESIGN RICHARD KAZARIAN ANTIQUES / PHOTO ERIC ROTH

SLEEP SECRETS

A LOW TEMPERATURE PROMOTES BETTER SLEEP, WHILE A WARM BEDROOM CAN ACTUALLY INTERFERE WITH SLEEP. THIS IS BECAUSE OUR BODY TEMPERATURE DROPS DURING SLEEP AND RISES AS OUR WAKING HOUR DRAWS NEAR. ACCORDING TO EXPERTS, THE IDEAL BEDROOM TEMPERATURE IS BETWEEN 65° AND 68°F (18° AND 20°C), BUT THAT WON'T SUIT EVERYONE. WOMEN USUALLY PREFER A SLIGHTLY WARMER ROOM TEMPERATURE THAN MEN, BUT IT'S EASIER FOR THE PERSON WHO IS COLD TO ADD A BLANKET THAN FOR THE PERSON WHO IS HOT TO COOL DOWN.

ABOVE If used astutely, one piece of furniture can evoke a style or period. Here, a modernist mood is established by the George Nelson bench, which is emphasized still further by the use of a color scheme that pays homage to the period.

DESIGN POWELL/KLEINSCHMIDT / PHOTO TONY BERARDI

OPPOSITE Blend the rough and the refined to create a space that is pristine and serene. Combine architectural elements that are both contemporary and antique, such as brick walls, a concrete floor, and a beamed wood ceiling with fresh white textiles, creamy translucent closet doors, and elegant warm wood furnishings.

DESIGN INSIGHT WEST / PHOTO DAVID GLOMB

An Asian ambience doesn't necessarily call for colloquial furnishings. A low-slung platform bed calls a futon to mind. Panels on the wall are reminiscent of a shoji screen; artworks propped against a wall are spare pieces that have an Eastern aesthetic; and an assortment of vases and a bowl are grouped together to mimic an appropriate tableau. Though all-American, the miniblinds emphasize the horizontal set of the space and have been used in a translucent hue that suggests washi.

PHOTO TIM STREET-PORTER

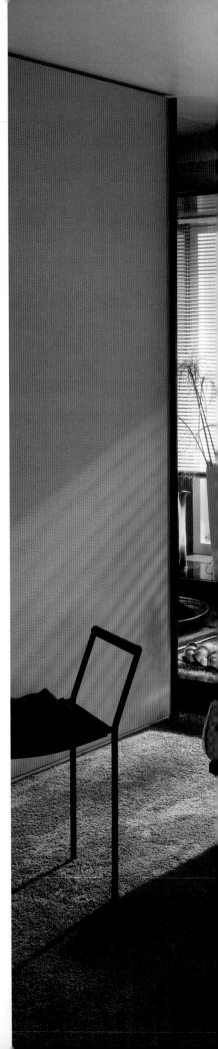

buying **linens**

LINENS COME IN EVERY INCARNATION, FROM FROTHY AND FINE TO RUSTIC AND ROUGH. FIBERS AND THREAD COUNTS VARY, ALONG WITH COSTS. SO IT'S POSSIBLE TO PIECE TOGETHER YOUR BED DRESSING, AND CREATE A SPECIFIC STYLE, BY COMBINING DIFFERENT ELEMENTS.

HERE'S WHAT TO KEEP IN MIND

- All cotton sheets soften with washing, while blends wrinkle less but aren't as soft. Pima and Egyptian cottons are extra lustrous and retain this sheen through repeated washings. Quality is indicated by thread count, which is the number of threads per square inch. Standard is 180 to 200, while 350 is luxurious.

- Mix and match to make a bed great by combining prints. The best principle to remember is that opposites attract. Curves should be balanced with straighter edges. For example, some perfect pairings are lush florals with simple stripes or linear geometrics with curvy designs.

- Save money by mixing less expensive solid sheets with designer prints, pillows with special trims or finishes, and elegant comforters. Duvet covers can be expensive, so make your own using two high-quality flat sheets (preferably bought on sale). Sew them together on all sides, leaving unsewn the center third of the fourth side, where you can add buttons, snaps, or ribbon ties.

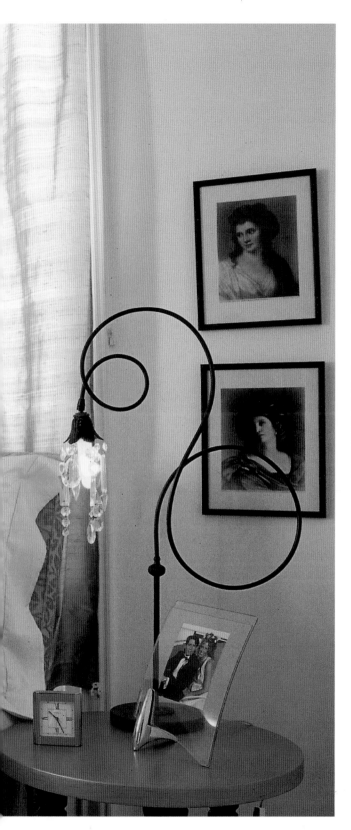

ABOVE Function and form coalesce in bedside lighting. This fanciful table lamp is a capricious counterpoint to the sumptuous but sedately dressed bed.

DESIGN M. J. FOREMAN / PHOTO TONY BERARDI

LEFT Take advantage of a room's natural attributes. When the bed is in an alcove created by large picture windows, the window treatment becomes a dramatic extension of the headboard. Gossamer drapes let in light but screen out the view for privacy.

DESIGN M. J. FOREMAN / PHOTO TONY BERARDI

havens for relaxation

THE LUXURY OF POSSESSING A ROOM THAT CAN BE DEVOTED SOLELY TO SLEEP IS NOT ENJOYED BY EVERYONE, SINCE WE TEND TO OCCUPY DIFFERENT TYPES OF LIVING QUARTERS AT EACH STAGE OF LIFE.

Young people often live in small studio apartments; families may have more members than bedrooms; and empty-nesters often condense their space to much smaller proportions. Lifestyles are also changing, and many of us work at home for some part of the week or full-time. Or we want to streamline our lives and eliminate the necessity to go out of our homes to work out or participate in hobbies.

Ultimately, these realities motivate us to combine a sleeping space with other activities. Today's bedrooms or guest rooms often incorporate studies, entertainment areas, home offices, or even gyms. Hence, we are seeing the advent of the double-duty room, a space that is decidedly devoted to two or more endeavors.

Yet the concept of using our bedrooms for two or even more activities is definitely not new. In fact, a room devoted solely to sleep is a relatively recent innovation in the historical scheme of things, made possible for the masses only by the Industrial Revolution. Before that time, only the very wealthy had homes large enough to accommodate a sleeping chamber. Most families slept together in communal rooms that were sometimes part of a large communal living space where all the activities of daily life took place.

So perhaps this trend toward the multipurpose bedroom can be seen as a return to our roots. But the types of double-duty spaces being designed today are far more effective and imaginative than ever before, thanks to many factors. We have the benefit of research that tells us how to structure these spaces for optimal performance. And the furniture industry has responded to our needs, creating a range of flexible furnishings that can fulfill more than one function, convert to another form, or be folded down and stashed away when not in use.

Shared spaces can be made all the more charming by clutter, but there are tricks to this technique. These are actually carefully crafted milieus with a meticulous organizational framework in place under all the layers. Witness the carefully stacked magazines, well-organized books, and bed unencumbered by any clutter in this inviting library-cum-bedroom.
PHOTO DAVID GLOMB

Of course, in every double-duty bedroom, the bed, a huge piece of furniture in its own right, must coexist with a range of other furnishings. A major consideration is whether or not the bed has to double as seating during the day, since this will determine the type of configuration it must take and how the room must be organized. In a large bedroom, a portion of the space that would otherwise go unused can be devoted to another activity, leaving the bed to fulfill its true calling. The extra space can assume its own identity by sheer square footage or furniture arrangement. For instance, a spacious bedroom can be endowed with a chaise, weights and mats, or a desk in an open corner, turning that expanse into a sitting area, gym, or home office. Or a set of shelves or a screen can be used to physically separate that area from the rest of the room.

In a sleeping space that is used everyday but must also double as a home office, entertainment area, or gym, the bed is still of critical importance and must be of the highest quality possible. Most sofa beds or foldaways aren't supportive enough to be used every night, but a bed can be camouflaged as a sofa with the use of a slipcover and plenty of pillows. Many beds with supportive mattresses are also designed as dual-purpose pieces. They double as seating or storage—or both—during the day, thanks to the way they are designed, but are still comfortable and sturdy enough to sleep on every night.

If a double-duty room is going to double as a guest room, a bevy of space-saving solutions will apply. Virtually any seating that doubles as a bed, such as a futon, sofa bed, daybed, couch, or trundle bed, can be employed depending on the size of the space and its design. If the space is truly tiny, keep in mind that a daybed or couch is much more space-efficient than a sofabed that needs to be opened for use. And don't discount the storage potential of a platform bed.

ABOVE & RIGHT If a room is extremely spacious, there's no necessity to set up physical barriers between activity centers. But it is important to keep everything in the same vein and make sure task areas have adequate lighting. A cohesive palette of caramels and creams is predominate in this room, and the reading area is located next to the windows to take advantage of natural light.

DESIGN JULA SUTTA / PHOTO COLIN MCRAE

SLEEP SECRETS

ACCENTUATE THE FOOT OF THE BED WITH A BENCH, A TRUNK, A LOW BUREAU, OR EVEN A STACK OF ANTIQUE LUGGAGE. DEPENDING ON THE PIECE, IT CAN ASSUME ANY DECORATIVE STYLE. IT WILL ALSO SERVE AS A PLACE TO SIT WHILE DRESSING, TO DROP CLOTHES ON, OR FOR STORAGE. IF THERE IS NO FOOTBOARD ON THE BED AND THE BED IS USED BY A TALL INDIVIDUAL, MAKE SURE THE TRUNK IS NO HIGHER THAN THE HEIGHT OF THE MATTRESS; OTHERWISE THE TRUNK WILL HAMPER FEET THAT PEEK OUT OVER THE EDGE OF THE BED.

Style and substance coalesce in this bedroom, where several techniques are used to physically divide the shared space. The square room is divided in two by both a one-step platform under the half that holds the bedroom and the placement of the furniture (the sitting area faces away from the bed). The four-poster bed is also fitted with heavy drapes that can close it off from the rest of the room, which lets two activities take place in the space at once.

PHOTO ERIC ROTH

flexible **furniture**

A BEDROOM MAY HAVE TO BE SHARED
BETWEEN SEVERAL ACTIVITIES, SUCH
AS DRESSING, RELAXING, STUDYING,
WORKING, AND EXERCISING—OR IT CAN
BE A GUEST ROOM THAT IS DEVOTED
TO OTHER PURSUITS WHEN VISITORS
AREN'T PRESENT. REMEMBER THAT A
BED TAKES UP A HUGE AMOUNT OF
FLOOR SPACE, SO MAKE SURE THE REST
OF THE FURNITURE IN THE ROOM
TRULY EARNS ITS KEEP.

HERE'S WHAT TO KEEP IN MIND

- Keep it compact. Smaller pieces of furniture have the ability to fit into tight or awkward spots. A bedside table can be tiny; it only has to hold a clock. To eke out storage in a small space, make a bedside table out of a storage cube or small chest. A stool or bench can supply the seating.

- Add wheels. Furniture that can easily be moved from one part of the room to another (or from room to room) can help make better use of the space. Put wheels on a chest or box so that it can become a coffee table by day and bed stand by night. Or add wheels to a table so that it can easily be rolled around the room to be used for a variety of activities. And don't forget portable storage, such as butler's trays or trolleys, for holding essentials. A whole home office, or all the essentials a guest will need, can be stored on these types of pieces and wheeled from spot to spot as needed.

- Fold it up or out. Furniture that folds can be used to create temporary space in a room. Create a seating area with a folding chair and stool, and flank it with a low folding table. Or opt for a folding chaise longue and cover it with a thick pad. An eating or working area can be set up with a folding table and chairs. Cover both with textiles (a pretty tablecloth and slipcovers or seat pads for the chairs) to increase their comfort and improve their appearance.

- Screen it off. To define the boundaries of a sleep, work, or dressing area, use a freestanding shelving unit, a bookcase, or a screen. All provide varying degrees of adaptability, since some are more mobile than others. A shelving unit can be equipped with wheels; if not, it must remain in place. But a screen can be easily moved and can be used to mask myriad problem spots. Use it in front of a bed for privacy, in front of a window instead of curtains, or merely to add decorative impact.

No matter how tight the area, there's always a way to carve out a little sitting space in a bedroom. An Eames rocker is lightweight enough to pick up and move to any available space, even if it's in front of an entryway or closet, while wheels make a chest of drawers mobile enough to push out of the way.

DESIGN LYNETTE HAND / PHOTO ERIC ROTH

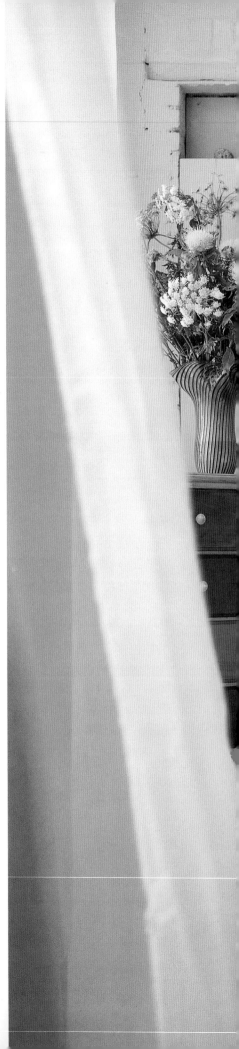

More is more in some instances. A brimming bookcase, plenty of seating, a foot stool, and a bed create the look of comfortable clutter.

PHOTO TIM STREET-PORTER

Blue is a cool, calm, and restful hue, often called the color of contemplation. That makes it the perfect choice for this beach house, which is loaded with spots for restful stolen moments.

DESIGN BENJAMIN NORIEGA-ORTIZ / PHOTO PETER MARGONELLI

ABOVE No matter how sleek, spare, or contemporary a space, a chaise longue begs for the right accessories. A soft throw or a cushy pillow are de rigueur.

DESIGN CAROL WOLK INTERIORS / PHOTO TONY BERARDI

OPPOSITE Color can be used to heighten the effect of a specific space. Since maroon is considered to be a subdued and cautious hue that encourages deep thoughtfulness, it's an ideal shade to use on a relaxing space.

PHOTO COURTESY OF SPIEGEL

SLEEP SECRETS

FOR SOME, IT IS NECESSARY TO MAKE THE BEDROOM AS DARK AS POSSIBLE, ESPECIALLY IN AN URBAN AREA WHERE THE CITY LIGHTS ARE BRIGHT AT NIGHT. INVEST IN GOOD SHADES IF YOU ARE SENSITIVE TO LIGHT. ON THE OTHER HAND, SUNLIGHT IS A POWERFUL INDICATOR TO OUR BODIES OF WHEN IT'S TIME TO GET UP AND CAN MAKE WAKING EASIER. WHEN LIGHT FALLS ON YOUR RETINA, IT TRIGGERS YOUR BODY CLOCK TO BEGIN A TWENTY-FOUR-HOUR CYCLE OF WAKEFULNESS AND SLEEP. ONE OPTION IS TO OPEN THE SHADES AS SOON AS THE ALARM GOES OFF TO ABSORB LIGHT AND GET GOING.

ABOVE When eclectic items are used in a space, color becomes a unifying factor. In the sitting area of this bedroom, the chairs have a traditional bent while the bed is thoroughly contemporary; they relate well thanks to the use of gray. A set of cold steel storage shelves mounted on wheels is tempered and given a timeless demeanor by a plush brown slipcover, which also relates to the Deco-style side table in the sitting area and tray table next to the bed.

PHOTO COURTESY OF SPIEGEL

LEFT To squeeze a home office into a bedroom, make shrewd use of every nook. Here, a desk is situated right in front of the windows, where the user can enjoy natural light, while the books are relegated to an alcove around the corner.

PHOTO COURTESY OF SPIEGEL

color

COLOR IS A POWERFUL TOOL IN DECORATING
THE BEDROOM, AS IT CAN BE EXPRESSIVE,
VERSATILE, AND INSPIRING. FURTHERMORE, ITS
EFFECTS HAVE BEEN SCIENTIFICALLY PROVEN TO
AFFECT PHYSICAL, PSYCHOLOGICAL, AND EMO-
TIONAL WELL-BEING. COLOR CAN BE USED TO
CREATE A RANGE OF MOODS THAT ENHANCES
THE WAY WE FUNCTION IN A SPECIFIC ROOM.
A SIMPLE COAT OF PAINT IS OFTEN ALL IT TAKES
TO TRANSFORM A ROOM, AND IS ALSO AN
EASY AND AFFORDABLE DECORATIVE DEVICE
TO EMPLOY.

EVERY COLOR HAS ITS OWN ATTRIBUTES.
YELLOW INCREASES EFFICIENCY, WHILE BLUE
SOOTHES THE NERVES AND INDUCES SLEEP. RED
IS STIMULATING AND DYNAMIC, WHILE GREEN
IS A HARMONIOUS COLOR THAT CAN BE
WELCOMING AND WARM.

TO USE A SPECIFIC COLOR OR A COMBINATION
OF HUES IN THE BEDROOM, IT IS IMPORTANT TO
TAKE THEIR PHYSICAL AND PSYCHOLOGICAL
EFFECTS INTO CONSIDERATION. SOME EXPERTS
EVEN BELIEVE ALL MENTAL, EMOTIONAL, AND
PHYSICAL PROBLEMS CAN BE ALLEVIATED
THOUGH THE USE OF COLOR IN OUR ENVIRON-
MENTS, SO CHOOSE COLORS FOR HOW THEY
AFFECT YOU.

HERE'S HOW

- Before choosing a color, think about whom the occupants will be and the effects the colors will have on them. Someone who has trouble getting up in the morning would benefit from a bright, sunny hue, while an overactive child would be best served by colors that instill a sense of calm.

- Take the size and shape of the bedroom into consideration. Stronger colors make a room seem smaller and more intense—and vice versa—and lighter ceilings make walls seem tall. Darker ceilings make a space seem smaller and more intimate.

- Warmer colors are usually easier to live with than cold colors, and familiarity breeds psychological contentment. For that reason, choose colors that you are comfortable with and that make you feel good. It often makes sense to stick to colors that are similar in value and tone to those you already know instead of following trends that are not in line with your taste.

- Look to coveted collections or favorite pieces of furniture or textiles to inspire your color scheme. For example, paint a sleep space in the soothing pale hues of blue or cream to complement a light wood bed frame.

- Colors reflect off each other, so if you choose to paint an entire wall a dark or vibrant shade, it will affect all the other colors in the room. For instance, as light bounces off a wall, it transfer the color of that wall to nearby objects and furnishings. So before introducing a strong hue into a room, paint it on a piece of plywood, and move the sample to different areas in the room over a period of several days. This will show you how the color relates to pieces in the room that will be close to the wall.

ABOVE Make every piece of furniture earn its keep, especially if space is at a premium. In the sitting area of this bedroom, an ottoman can be used as either a footrest or coffee table.

PHOTO COURTESY OF SPIEGEL

RIGHT There are many devices that can be used to define two separate areas in the same space, but translucent glass panels and/or screens are among the most effective. They let natural light shine through but still provide enough camouflage to establish a sense of privacy between two areas. Best of all, they can be fabricated in a wide range of designs, such as these wood-edged panels.

PHOTO COURTESY OF SPIEGEL

ABOVE In the East, residences rarely have enough space to devote a whole room to sleep. Instead, neutral surroundings become a bedroom when a futon is unfurled. The same premise is at work in this room, which has been designed with Eastern aesthetics in mind.

PHOTO TIM STREET-PORTER

LEFT Turn a corner into a hub of inactivity by outfitting it with everything you need to relax. Consider a good reading lamp, space for lots of books, side tables to hold beverages or snacks, cushy pillows, and a warm throw.

PHOTO COURTESY OF SPIEGEL

siestas

In a room scheme, a daybed is a large piece of furniture. Thanks to its scale and proportion, it can be used as more than just a place to sit or lay down. Position it as a partition in a large or open space to divide or emphasize two distinct activity areas.

DESIGN BENJAMIN NORIEGA-ORTIZ /
PHOTO PETER MARGONELLI

EVERYBODY NEEDS A PLACE TO PUT UP HIS OR HER FEET AND RELAX, WHETHER IT'S TO SIT QUIETLY AND READ, GAZE AT THE SCENERY OUTSIDE, OR GRAB A SHORT NAP—IN ESSENCE, SOMEWHERE TO ESCAPE THE STRESSES OF DAILY LIFE.

While a whole room devoted to this pursuit would be ideal, it is often unrealistic, given the space constraints most of us have. So it is necessary to carve out an ideal refuge from places that already exist within our homes.

This sort of space can be carved out of the corner of a room, be it a bedroom, study, family room, or home office. The only requisite is a bit of seclusion, which can be achieved with decorative devices ranging from folding screens to shelving systems when necessary, although it also helps to have natural light and decent views. Furnish this space with sensuous pieces, such as a cushy recliner or a sinuous chaise longue. Or use exotic trappings that will make it into a singular escape within your own home, such as a hammock or porch swing hung inside to bring the outdoors in.

Don't ignore the spaces outside your home. In good weather, transform a corner of a balcony, deck, or yard into a spot for peaceful repose or a siesta. Set a deck chair under an awning or tree, spread a blanket on the grass, or hang a hammock somewhere in the yard. Instead of searching for something special, use comfortable indoor furniture that has already seen better days but still has enough life to withstand the elements for a while. Position these pieces so that they can catch the sun or take advantage of any view.

Ultimately, siesta spaces need to possess the right levels of comfort and illumination. The seating should be substantial and supportive so that it can nurture and sustain for reasonable lengths of time. The lighting must be adaptable so that it can easily be adjusted to accommodate a range of activities.

Fortunately, there are many types of furnishings that can be used to achieve these goals. Seating can take many forms, be it cozy armchairs paired with ottomans or footstools, posture-conscious recliners, pragmatic daybeds, glamorous chaise longues, or even an inviting pile of cushions thrown on the floor. Lamps or torchères can be positioned in these spaces for optimal effect, especially if they're outfitted with adjustable shades and dimmers.

Once a retreat is carved out of a room, the last step is to imbue it with a sense of calm and enclosure. Here's where personal preference matters most, since this may involve paring down the space to bare essentials or surrounding oneself with cherished belongings. Sound can also be a factor in the last part of this process, since everyone has a different tolerance level. One person can sleep with the television or stereo on, while another needs perfect silence. Situate a retreat right next to a window to catch the soothing sounds of the world outside. There is always a way to find the right siesta spot in a home.

ABOVE Take advantage of a spectacular view with a window seat. Plump pillows make it the perfect spot for a siesta, while a slim lamp will provide enough light for reading at night.
PHOTO TONY BERARDI

OPPOSITE A chaise longue or daybed gives a room a restful demeanor that is still fairly formal, yet it can also do double duty as a bed. Here, a rich lacquered chest with an Oriental motif gives the whole setting an Eastern aesthetic and doubles as storage if a guest uses the room.
PHOTO DAVID GLOMB

SLEEP SECRETS

CONTRARY TO POPULAR OPINION, CATCHING A NAP IN THE AFTERNOON DOESN'T MEAN SLACKING OFF. HUMANS HAVE A BIOLOGICAL NEED FOR A MIDDAY DOZE BECAUSE WE EVOLVED FROM INHABITANTS OF REGIONS AROUND THE EQUATOR. THERE, HOT AFTERNOONS INDUCED LETHARGY AND DEVELOPED THE PATTERN OF NAPPING. REGARDLESS, RESEARCH DOES SHOW THAT A QUICK AFTERNOON NAP CAN IMPROVE WAKEFULNESS AND INCREASE EFFICIENCY. TO AVOID POST-NAP GROGGINESS, THE OPTIMAL LENGTH OF TIME IS THIRTY MINUTES.

The corner of a room isn't usually big enough to hold enough seating to turn it into a conversation area. All it takes is the right chair, accompanied by a few critical accessories, such as a reading lamp and lavish throw, to transform it into a the perfect spot for a brief respite.

PHOTO ERIC ROTH

ABOVE Everyone has a favorite spot in a room that they embrace as their own, which can get tricky if two people covet the same spot. A matched set arranged as mirror opposites also encourages a bit of togetherness.

DESIGN BENJAMIN NORIEGA-ORTIZ / PHOTO PETER MARGONELLI

LEFT Reading and napping are two of life's greatest pleasures. When planning a library, make sure there are plenty of opportunities to accomplish both feats. Besides sumptuous chairs and an ottoman, there's a window seat with a reading lamp featured in this library.

DESIGN LESLIE JONES DESIGN / PHOTO DOUG SNOWER PHOTOGRAPHY

Color and light can play off each other to warm up even the most minimal room. A warm cast from a wall sconce and the fire reflecting off the sienna walls and waxed parquet floor create an alluring and calming glow.

DESIGN ANTONIO CITTERIO, B & B ITALIA / PHOTO COURTESY OF LUMINAIRE

creating siesta **spaces**

THERE ARE MANY WAYS TO RECLAIM A BIT OF HOME SPACE TO BE USED FOR SIESTAS. MINE LEFTOVER SPACES, SUCH AS THE HOLLOW BENEATH THE EAVES, AN ODD ALCOVE, THE ECCENTRIC LANDING AT THE TOP OF THE STAIRS, OR ANY DEAD SPACES IN THE CORNERS OF ROOMS. OR CONDENSE A SUITE OF FURNISHINGS IN A ROOM BY PUSHING THEM A LITTLE CLOSER TOGETHER, AND DIVIDE THE SPACE WITH A PARTITION. CONSIDER USING FOLDING SCREENS, LARGE SHELVING UNITS, CURTAINS ON RODS, OR EVEN THE WAY FURNISHINGS ARE POSITIONED TO CREATE A RELAXING SIESTA SPACE.

COMFORT ALWAYS COMES FIRST. LOOK
FOR A CHAIR, RECLINER, SOFA, CHAISE
LONGUE, OR DAYBED THAT WILL GIVE ALL
THE SUPPORT AND COMFORT NEEDED.
IDEALLY, ONE SHOULD BE ABLE TO SIT
UPRIGHT, RECLINE IN SOME FORM, AND
EASILY MANIPULATE THE SEAT TO
CHANGE POSITIONS. IF THE SEATING
FALLS SHORT IN ANY WAY, AN OTTOMAN
OR STOOL FOR FOOT SUPPORT CAN BE
USED, AS WELL AS PILLOWS OR BOLSTERS
FOR THE BACK.

FLEXIBLE FURNISHINGS ARE IDEAL FOR
THIS PURPOSE. LOOK FOR ENTERTAIN-
MENT CENTERS THAT CAN BE WHEELED
AWAY, CHAIRS THAT CAN BE ROLLED AND
EASILY ADJUSTED, A SOFA WITH A TRUN-
DLE BED THAT CAN BE PULLED OUT AT
WILL, OR ADAPTABLE TABLES THAT CAN
HOLD DRINKS OR READING MATERIALS.

If possible, a perfect spot for a siesta is the bedroom, away from the action of everyday life. This bedroom adjoins a study and already has plenty of reading materials close at hand; adding a striking chaise longue adds more energy to the style of the space.

PHOTO TIM STREET-PORTER

ABOVE LEFT Relaxing alfresco rivals dining alfresco; the fresh air makes you long for more. Plump cushions on the loungers and an umbrella to screen out the ultraviolet rays are basic necessities in this situation.

PHOTO COURTESY OF SPIEGEL

LEFT Take advantage of a spectacular backyard setting—especially one that involves landscaped foliage. Outfit it with furnishings that will allow resting or reading.

DESIGN INSIGHT WEST / PHOTO DAVID GLOMB

RIGHT Use the concept of a siesta by the shore indoors. Find a serene spot to set up a folding chair and relax for a while. The setting can be semipermanent, rotated with other furnishings as desired.

PHOTO COURTESY OF EXPOSURES

Soft cotton slipcovers can increase the comfort quotient of a sofa or ottoman by covering up an uncomfortable fabric underneath. It can also give these pieces a new lease on life by lightening them up for the summer months, or the reverse.

DESIGN BENJAMIN NORIEGA-ORTIZ / PHOTO PETER MARGONELLI

SLEEP SECRETS

ONE OF THE EASIEST WAYS TO GET A SPECIAL SPOT FOR RELAXING OR CATCHING A NAP IS TO CARVE IT OUT OF THE BEDROOM. MOST OF THE ESSENTIALS ARE ALREADY IN PLACE; THEY JUST NEED TO BE REARRANGED OR AUGMENTED A BIT. MOVE AN EASY CHAIR TO A CORNER OF THE BEDROOM AND PAIR IT WITH AN OTTOMAN OR STOOL. ADD A FLOOR LAMP AND SIDE TABLE, AND A RESTFUL TABLEAU IS COMPLETE. TURN THE CHAIR SO THAT IT'S FACING A WINDOW—OR IF SPACE ALLOWS, USE A LOVE SEAT SO THAT TWO CAN ENJOY THE SPACE AT THE SAME TIME.

ABOVE Turn a resplendent outdoor setting into the perfect spot to take a siesta with portable loungers. Covering them with thick cushions to make them softer is a must, as is utilizing a protective umbrella.

PHOTO COURTESY OF POTTERY BARN

LEFT What could be more soothing than a siesta by the shore? A folding cot, a few pillows, and a blanket or throw are all it takes—and best of all they're quite portable.

PHOTO COURTESY OF EXPOSURES

ABOVE An easy way to increase the style in tiny nooks is to use a pattern or motif, such as a lace curtain. Beds that are tucked into corners provide a feeling of intimacy that can enhance the sleep experience.

DESIGN LISA JACKSON / PHOTO DAVID GLOMB

OPPOSITE No matter how casual a space happens to be, there are ways to increase its siesta quotient. Huge pillows stacked on the floor can be used as is or spread out, while a platform topped with a mattress can function as a sofa or bed. All make appropriate spots in which to nap.

PHOTO TIM STREET-PORTER

Texture, shape, and hue can be used to suggest a specific style rather than the pieces of furniture. A low-slung, spare chaise flanked by side tables of the same ilk evoke an Eastern ambience, which is enhanced by ethnic art with a similar aesthetic.

PHOTO DAVID GLOMB

ABOVE A breathtaking landscape is always an inducement to sit and ponder the scene outside, so locate a chaise in an appropriate spot. The Eastern aesthetic in this room helps matters further by matching the scenery outside with its spare mood.

DESIGN ANTONIO CITTERIO / PHOTO COURTESY OF LUMINAIRE

RIGHT Don't hesitate to treat a daybed like a sofa or chair. Accessorize it with other furnishings. Pairing it with an end table situated in its center instead of at either end visually cuts its length down to a more proportionate size and increases its practicality.

PHOTO COURTESY OF SPIEGEL

FOLLOWING PAGES A bed tucked into the corner of a room instantly provides a feeling of intimacy that invites napping. Pure white linens make it seem sensuous, fresh, and a bit more spacious, especially if it's bordered by a window. Increase the style quotient of such a tiny nook by adding a pattern or motif, such as a lace curtain.

DESIGN BRAD BLAIR / PHOTO DAVID GLOMB

bedroom retreats

THE BEDROOM IS NOT MEANT TO BE A ROOM ON SHOW IN THE HOME.

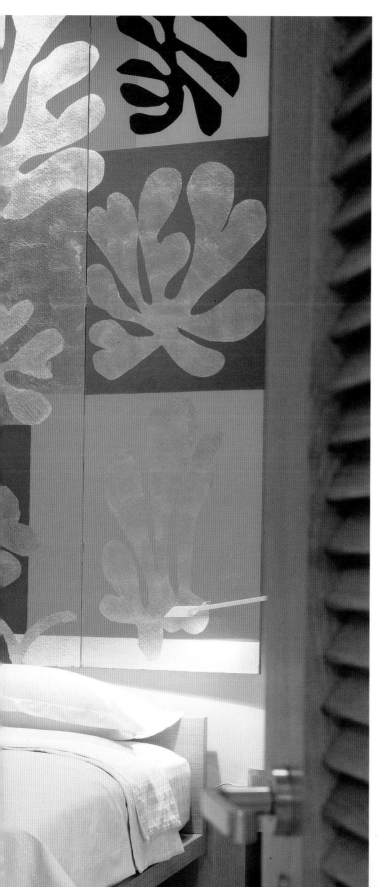

Yet precisely because it is such a private space and usually situated away from the public areas of the home, it can be decorated with a little more indulgence and a lot less practicality than other rooms. That means the sky's the limit. This is one place in the house where you can be original, imaginative, fanciful, or even extravagant or flamboyant.

Instead of just worrying about the basics, such as an adequate sleeping surface and ample storage, focus on your personality and your dreams. Fill this room with the things you treasure or admire, indulge your whims, and let your imagination run wild. Do you want a quirky furnishing to take center stage? Perhaps you want to create a secretive and lairlike hideaway, or transform this room into an oasis of serenity, or even the reverse—revamp the room with riotous color. It's entirely up to you.

A bedroom retreat can house collections of every ilk, be it superb and finely honed or quirky and casually accumulated. For instance, a hoard of vintage purses or clusters of globes can be just as remarkable and vital to the mood of a room as a collection of fine art or elegant objects such as boxes or crystal paperweights. This also challenges the notion that beautiful displays are intended mostly for show and are wasted on us alone. Have fun with design in your bedroom—defy convention. In lieu of a bedspread, use an exotic or unexpected textile on the bed. Start with a plain duvet in a strong neutral tone, then top it with a rug, a shawl, an Indian blanket, a table runner, or even a length of cloth with an attractive border. Change the textile to change the nature of the room.

Keep in mind that a sleeping retreat doesn't have to be relegated to the rooms inside your home. If you have access to a balcony or roof with a spectacular view and the energy to transform it into a retreat on a temporary basis—as weather permits—go ahead and give it a try.

Ultimately, the bedroom can be as novel, eclectic, dramatic, luxurious, exotic, or eccentric as you like. This is the one place in your home where

Placement is everything in this astutely designed bedroom. Spare, low-slung furnishings in neutral hues are designed to induce sleep at night and a graphic, dynamic screen that's visible only out of bed is contrived to rouse sleepers by day.
PHOTO DAVID GLOMB

LEFT (Detail) Substance and style coalesce in the details, such as a Deco-inspired night table and luxurious bedding. Though ultimately functional as accessories go, these chic items also add a tremendous amount of style to the space.
PHOTO COURTESY OF SPIEGEL

RIGHT An alcove that is just large enough to envelop a bed precludes the need for a headboard or high-performance nightstand. To store necessities such as an alarm clock and reading materials and to anchor adequate lighting so that you can read in bed, install built-in shelves.
PHOTO COURTESY OF SPIEGEL

it is possible to stretch the limits. No decorative treatment is impossible to employ with the right perspective. Be resourceful with the way you employ paint, wallpaper, and textiles. These are basically just tools to manipulate to achieve your dreams.

Paint can be wielded in many ways, from textural or dimensional surfaces that are created with faux finishes to astonishingly real imagery that calls upon techniques such as trompe l'oeil. Thanks to many new printing technologies, wallpapers can mimic the same effects and finishes, often much more inexpensively. Don't rule out textiles, such as in a tented or shirred room or to use as an accent or finishing touch to other treatments.

Fantasy is about making the impossible come true. The trick to fulfilling your fantasies is to bring them into the world that is part of your daily life. For sources of inspiration, look to periods or styles from the past, foreign or exotic places you've visited, pictures from magazines, or even films. A painting by a favorite artist or a favorite romantic vacation spot may motivate you to pay homage to these forces with the decor of your bedroom.

Whatever you choose to create or achieve in your dream room, it must reflect your own personal aesthetics and desires. When designing this sort of bedroom, let your dreams be your guide. With this approach, it will become much more than a place to sleep—a private, peaceful, and sustaining retreat.

SLEEP SECRETS

YOUR BEDROOM CAN BE A HAVEN FOR YOUR MOST INTIMATE OR FAVORED PURSUITS. WHO SAYS HOBBIES MUST BE RELEGATED TO OTHER CORNERS OF OUR HOUSEHOLD? IF PAINTING IS YOUR PASSION, A BEDROOM CAN HOUSE A SMALL STUDIO, OR AN AVID GARDENER CAN GROW APPROPRIATE HOUSEPLANTS IN THE BEDROOM.

ABOVE A shared bedroom can still have enough cachet and allure to make it special for everyone who uses it. Diaphanous fabric on twin four-poster beds and casement windows, a soaring ceiling, a monochromatic color scheme, and a cozy window seat all raise the style and comfort quotients of this bedroom so much that it is undeniably a striking sanctuary for its occupants.

DESIGN KALMAN CONSTRUCTION / PHOTO ERIC ROTH

RIGHT Often there's room to carve out an entire personal retreat under the eaves. Here, skylights flood the space with light and make it seem much larger than it is, and the use of low, horizontal furnishings finishes the job. Partitions that seclude a bit of the bed give the sleeping space the illusion of being a whole other room.

DESIGN BRAD BLAIR / PHOTO DAVID GLOMB

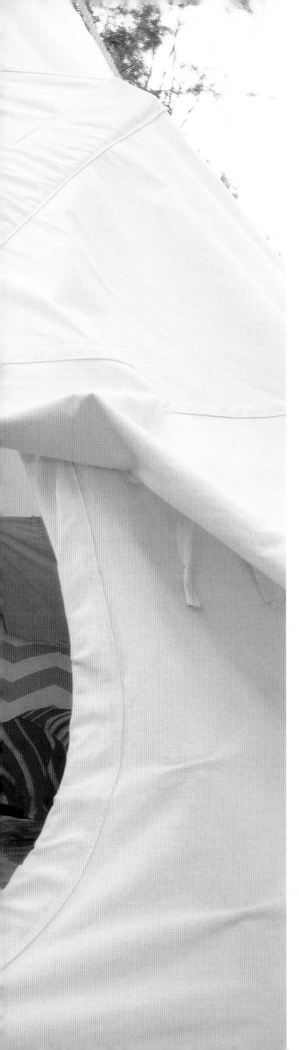

ABOVE A tent can be lavished with the same sort of luxurious or wondrous decorative touches you would use in a room, such as opulent textiles or an extraordinary chandelier.

DESIGN INSIGHT WEST / PHOTO DAVID GLOMB

LEFT When you lack enough room to fulfill a fantasy, or just want a remarkable change of pace, consider using the space outside your home. With all the right trappings, a tent can become the sleeping retreat of your dreams.

DESIGN INSIGHT WEST / PHOTO DAVID GLOMB

creating your
bedroom retreat

- Be creative and bold with decorative elements. Don't hesitate to try integrating daring color combinations, over-the-top patterns, or unusual textures into the mix. When employing these novel treatments, remember that it pays to try something cost-effective first. Create the mood with fanciful or vibrant linens that can be easily changed, or a wall-spanning drape in a wild pattern that can be pulled to one side on occasion.

- Add all the amenities you crave. If you love music, invest in a superior sound system; if you want to eat or drink in the space, consider that mini refrigerator, espresso machine, or wet bar.

- Use lighting as a tool. Vital to the atmosphere of the room, lighting can be used to create different effects at different times. It can be targeted to accent a certain feature in the room, such as a coveted collection, or to create a mood, be it exhilarating or relaxed. For optimal results, outfit the room with several types of lighting and equip the basic system for the room with dimmers, since they can be used to change the mood to suit the moment.

- Don't forget the basics; function must still be a priority. No matter how singular, eclectic, elegant, or fantastical the furnishings, they still must be practical and offer up all the comfort and sustenance you need. Make sure you have a comfortable, supportive bed, adequate lighting and ventilation, and enough storage to accommodate your possessions.

Give a sleeper sofa the royal treatment to transform a double-duty room, such as a den or home office, into a nurturing retreat. Plain poles uphold a very simple yet extremely effective canopy, industrial scaffolds support reading lamps, and wheels on the bed table make it easy to shift around the room. Everything is lightweight and portable, ready to move back into place.

PHOTO TIM STREET-PORTER

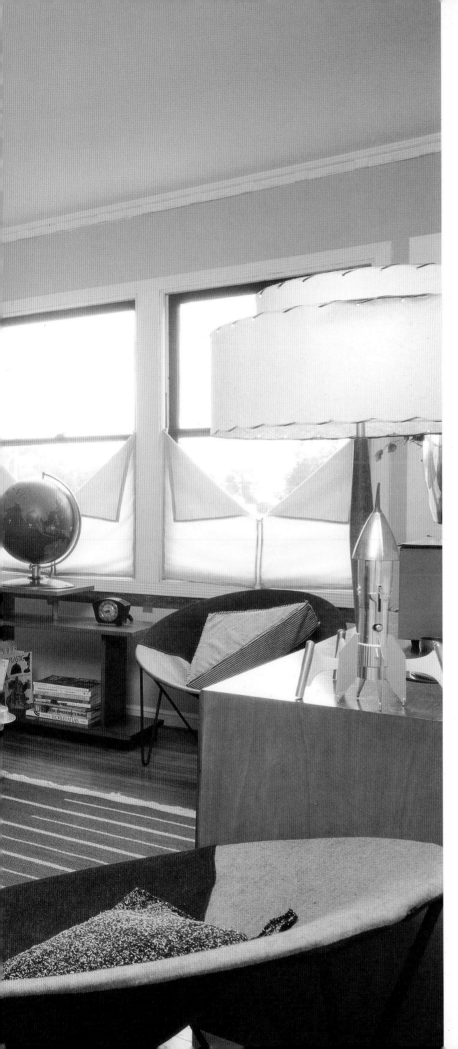

ABOVE A private retreat is the one area of your home where you can be as lavish or restrained as you wish with no one to pass judgment. Be inventive; an imaginative and lavish bed treatment such as this one, which is pieced together from contemporary and antique components and sports wheels for mobility, can totally transform the room from typical to extraordinary.

DESIGN BRIAN MURPHY / PHOTO TIM STREET-PORTER

LEFT Let the bedroom reflect your attachment to a particular period or style. Here, a midcentury aesthetic is evoked by an eclectic mixture of pieces that are both from that period and new. A few special touches steal the show, such as a collection of vintage globes.

DESIGN KACY AND MARK MARCINIK / PHOTO COLIN MCRAE

SLEEP SECRETS

ADD CASTERS TO THE BEDFRAME SO THAT IT CAN BE MOVED AROUND THE ROOM AS THE MOOD STRIKES YOU OR TO TAKE ADVANTAGE OF THE NATURAL RESOURCES OF THE SPACE. FOR INSTANCE, TO WAKE UP TO NATURAL LIGHT, MOVE THE BED NEXT TO THE WINDOW. TO USE THE BEDROOM FOR WORKING OUT, CLEAR A LARGE SPACE IN THE ROOM BY MOVING THE BED TO ONE SIDE.

Make the most of an architecturally significant space by using it for more than just sleep. By creating various activity areas in this bedroom, such as a lounging area for relaxing and reading and a work area with a table and chairs, the soaring space becomes a full-blown retreat instead of just a bedroom.

DESIGN INSIGHT WEST / PHOTO DAVID GLOMB

An outside space can become a bedroom retreat in the right climate with the right furnishings. Sea grass mats attached to the ceiling hug the four-poster bed and give it the impression of being fully dressed. For more privacy, or warmth if the temperature drops, fabric can be hung from its rods.

PHOTO COURTESY OF THE MORSON COLLECTION

history of the **bed**

SINCE BEDS WERE ONCE PILES OF STRAW STACKED ON THE FLOOR, THE EXPRESSION "HITTING THE HAY" MAKES SENSE. BY THE RENAISSANCE PERIOD, BEDS RANGED FROM PORTABLE BENCHLIKE PLANKS OF WOOD COVERED WITH BEDCLOTHES AND TOPPED WITH CANOPIES TO ELABORATELY CARVED WOODEN AFFAIRS, SOMETIMES BUILT INTO ALCOVES OR GIVEN CUPBOARDLIKE CONFIGURATIONS WITH POSTS AND CURTAINLIKE HANGINGS THAT LENT THEM THE PRIVACY AND WARMTH NECESSARY IN LARGE ROOMS USED AS LIVING QUARTERS BY DAY AND SLEEPING SPACES BY NIGHT.

EVENTUALLY, BEDS BECAME EXTREMELY LARGE, NOT ONLY TO HOLD NUMEROUS OCCUPANTS SINCE SEVERAL FAMILY MEMBERS OFTEN SLEPT TOGETHER, BUT TO CREATE GRAND IMPRESSIONS SINCE HAVING A ROOM DEVOTED TOTALLY TO SLEEPING WAS A SIGN OF GREAT WEALTH.

EVENTUALLY, BEDS SHRUNK TO MORE INTIMATE SIZES AS INDUSTRIALIZATION SPURRED THE BIRTH OF THE BONA FIDE BEDROOM. THE FACT THAT MODERN-DAY BEDS RANGE FROM FUTONS TO DRAPED AND CANOPIED NUMBERS PROVES THAT STYLES DO COME FULL CIRCLE.

THE WAY WE DRESS OUR BEDS HAS BEEN INFLU-ENCED BY CENTURIES OF STYLE, AND SINCE HISTORY REPEATS ITSELF, A BRIEF SURVEY OF THESE STYLES OFFERS A WEALTH OF DECORATING IDEAS. CONSIDER THE PILLOW: LUXURIOUS DOWN-STUFFED VERSIONS GO BACK TO ANCIENT ROME, WHILE PIL-ING ON SCADS OF THEM IS A PRACTICE APPROPRI-ATED FROM THE MIDDLE EAST. IN ANCIENT EGYPT, BEDS WERE OFTEN DRAPED WITH FISHING NETS TO KEEP OUT INSECTS, WHILE IN PROVINCIAL HOMES THROUGHOUT EUROPE, MATTRESSES COVERED IN EARTHY HOMESPUN OR TICKING WERE PLACED DIRECTLY ON THE FLOOR. TODAY'S STYLES PAY HOMAGE TO THESE DEVELOPMENTS. FOR INSTANCE, THE CURTAINED AND CANOPIED BEDS RECALL THE ENGLISH FOUR-POSTER, THE FUTON IS REMINISCENT OF JAPAN, THE DUVET IS DERIVED FROM FRENCH TRADITION, AND THE EIDERDOWN COMFORTER CAME FROM SWITZERLAND AND GERMANY.

HOW WE DRESS OUR BEDS NOW RELATES TO THE DESIGN OF THE ROOM, BUT REGARDLESS OF STYLE THESE TRAPPINGS MUST ALSO PROMOTE COMFORT. OTHERWISE, THE BED HAS NOT BEEN DRESSED FOR SUCCESS.

ABOVE Simplicity can breed the suspense necessary to make a bedroom retreat dramatic. These bold, sculptural furnishings are made all the more impressive by the use of space and textiles in the room. The sleeping area is situated in front of a huge picture window, which is manipulated to conceal or reveal light thanks to its two-tier fabrication (the sheers reveal while the heavy silk conceals).

DESIGN MONIQUE AND SERGIO SAVARESE / PHOTO COURTESY OF DIALOGICA

RIGHT Surround yourself with art in your bedroom. It's actually the room where you spend the most time, and living with your favorite pieces will have a positive impact on your spirit. It helps to have a bed that's just as artistic as the work on the walls.

DESIGN MONIQUE AND SERGIO SAVARESE / PHOTO COURTESY OF DIALOGICA

ABOVE Use color and fabric to make a simple space remarkable and add decorative panache to plain furnishings. Bold yellow walls add drama and depth to the room, while a graphically arresting bed crown gives a routine bed all the glamour of a full-blown four-poster.

PHOTO ERIC ROTH

LEFT Fabric and paint can be used to play out your fantasies. A trompe l'oeil paint treatment on the walls emulates intricate moldings, while yards of alabaster cotton are used to dress up an already theatrical bed and vanity. Though these furnishings are opulent and formal, the same tactics can work with pieces of other decorative styles.

DESIGN KATE STAMPS / PHOTO TIM STREET-PORTER

ABOVE Where climates permit an outdoor room to be used year-round, it makes sense to furnish an outdoor retreat with substantial and extremely comfortable pieces of furniture. In just such a setting, this *lit á l'anglaise* with Oriental styling can function as a sofa or bed, and becomes both more functional and enchanting swathed in gossamer mosquito netting.

PHOTO TIM STREET-PORTER

RIGHT In lieu of fussy furnishings, use color and pattern to establish contrast and suggest texture. Simple pieces with rich, dark hues make the perfect counterpoint and temper the drama.

DESIGN INSIGHT WEST / PHOTO DAVID GLOMB

ABOVE To add texture, dimension, and elegance to walls, the renowned interior designer Sister Parish would cover them with

small squares of silver tea paper that imbued them with a sumptuous reflective quality. This modern-day version uses bigger

pieces of paper but employs the same trick to add depth, opulence, and drama to a relatively small, simply furnished space.

Snowy linens with a subtle scallop and fluffy down bed dressings add a chaste touch that balances the composition.

DESIGN BARBARA BARRY / PHOTO TIM STREET-PORTER

OPPOSITE Use an easy yet elegant decorative treatment, such as framing the bed in filmy netting, to lend more privacy and

panache to the bedroom. The impact of this device is so effective that it pays to leave the double doors to the bedroom open—

the view into this enticing bedroom retreat enhances the allure of the living room.

DESIGN BENJAMIN NORIEGA-ORTIZ / PHOTO PETER MARGONELLI

ABOVE A beautiful garden or yard makes it possible to retreat to the world outside your home. A chaise longue makes it alluring, especially one covered with a comfortable slipcover.

DESIGN BENJAMIN NORIEGA-ORTIZ / PHOTO PETER MARGONELLI

RIGHT When weather permits, turn a rooftop with a spectacular view of the sea into a sleeping retreat. In this case, the table, chairs, and stove are weatherproof, and a transparent railing allows the view of the city and sea to be prominent from every angle. The pillows and carpet lend the setting an exotic ethnic ambience.

DESIGN BRAD BLAIR / PHOTO DAVID GLOMB

SLEEP SECRETS

ABOUT THIRTY PERCENT OF THE GENERAL POPULATION SUFFERS FROM INSOMNIA—A PRETTY STAGGERING FIGURE. SOME OF THE BEST WAYS TO COMBAT INSOMNIA INCLUDE KEEPING ON A REGULAR SLEEP SCHEDULE, GETTING OUT OF BED WHEN YOU CAN'T SLEEP, AND AVOIDING ALCOHOL AND CAFFEINE IN THE EVENING.

Something as simple as a well-edited color scheme becomes a soothing retreat from everyday life. Combine a clean-lined, contemporary asthetic, with rustic styling. A handsome colonial bureau, beadboard walls, and assorted decorative accessories with a country demeanor are paired with a tailored bed.

DESIGN BENJAMIN NORIEGA-ORTIZ /
PHOTO PETER MARGONELLI

ABOVE Layers of textured linen in seascape colors of sky blue and shades of ecru create a reassuring atmosphere for retreat, and transform the whole room into a much more daring yet refined milieu.

DESIGN BENJAMIN NOREIGA-ORTIZ / PHOTO PETER MARGONELLI

RIGHT Bold wall shelves house an elegant collection of vases in this bedroom retreat.

PHOTO COURTESY OF SPIEGEL

Afterword

BY RISTOMATTI RATIA

Sleep is unequivocally one of life's greatest pleasures, for nothing is more gratifying than a good sleep, whether it lasts the whole night or is just a short nap. I always find the latter, those stolen moments where we doze in and out of wakefulness and ponder some pressing issue or merely reflect on life, the most satisfying form of sleep there is.

There are a number of cherished places in my life where I have been able to experience nurturing and sustained sleep. Our family estate in Porvoo, on the gulf of Finland, has a boathouse made of weathered pine logs that stretches out to the sea. Just inside its walls, but facing the sea, is a room that holds a glorious wood and canvas hammock designed by Aino Aalto, Alvar's wife. There, you can hear the wind rippling through the reeds and the water, and smell the salty air of the sea—elements that make this an intoxicating place to nap. On another part of the estate, there is a four-story windmill with a secret room on the top floor. All it contains is a simple bed—just a mattress on top of a platform. But it overlooks a magnificent vista of pine trees that sway in the wind and release their fragrant scent, making this a highly romantic and quixotic spot.

I have also created a number of spaces and accessories to facilitate this sort of sleep, starting with the first bedroom I had without my brother as a roommate when I was fourteen. It was in our apartment in Helsinki, and I decorated it with yards of sheer, silk screened fabric that I draped all over the room. It ended up on the cover of *Hopeapeili,* our most acclaimed lifestyle magazine at the time in Finland. Next, in the late sixties and early seventies, I put innovative motifs on sheets for Marimekko when I developed a bedding line for the company that was based on boldly colored, high-contrast stripes. This was at the time when solids and florals reigned supreme in the industry. Years later, in 1979, I designed my version of a fantasy bed, a tented canvas structure for *Seventeen* magazine, which had side panels that could be lifted or lowered, shelves on the edge of the roof-line, and storage ledges all around it. Much to my surprise, the magazine had 11,000 requests for the bed, proving that an alluring fantasy appeals to all.

The spaces we use for sleeping should be shrines to our personal needs and preferences, and places where we can create a secret world, make a statement or seek sanctuary. And we can learn how to design the spaces to fulfill these needs with forethought, planning, and action. In light of this reality, I commend *Sleeping Spaces* as a volume that can offer many concepts on the subject, and make it possible to help you understand what you want or need in your own bedrooms or places of respite. It will empower you to create the perfect domain, or perhaps a series of domains, in your home to facilitate and nurture sleep.

Ristomatti Ratia, a designer who worked with his family's company, Marimekko, from 1970 until 1983, has spent his whole career designing products for lifestyles and interiors. He began his career in 1966 as an interior architect, but turned to designing innovative products for mass production in 1969. Ratia made waves in the design world in the 1970s with his modular plastic Palaset cubes, which stacked to become a customized, do-it-yourself wall system and won the Scandinavian Design Award in 1973.

Ratia became vice president and creative director of Marimekko in 1973 and chairman of the board in 1979. He resigned in 1983, and went on to found his own international firm that creates designs produced by companies around the world. In the United States, his designs have been produced by Hold Everything, Crate & Barrel, Fitz & Floyd, Silvestri Corp., Motif Designs, and Design Ideas. Presently based in Finland and operating under the name Idea Factory, Ratia designs children's clothing, art glass, glassware, tabletop pieces, and home furnishings that are being produced by over twenty companies.

ARCHITECTS AND DESIGNERS

Barbara Barry
9526 Pico Boulevard
Los Angeles, CA 90035
310-276-9977

Mike Bell
1869 Merchandise Mart
Chicago, IL 60654
312-644-6848

Alessandra Branca
Branca
1325 N. State Parkway
Chicago, IL 60610
312-787-6123

Burns & Beyerl
601 S. LaSalle St., Ste. 300
Chicago, IL 60605
312-663-0222

Du Bay and Maire
445 N. Wells St.
Chicago, IL 60610
312-222-0445

Lonn L. Frye
Frye Gillan Molinaro Architects, Ltd.
308 W. Erie St., Ste. 600
Chicago, IL 60610
312-440-1584
fgmarch@aol.com

Shelly Handman
Handman Associates
222 W. Huron St.
Chicago, IL 60610
312-951-8456

Stephen Harby, Architect
718 Cedar Street
Santa Monica, CA 90405
310-450-8239

Anne Kaplan & Bruce Goers
Insight Environmental Designs
1997 Lake Ave.
Highland Park, IL 60035
847-432-4606

Bruce Goers, Wayne Williamson & Sam Cardella
Insight West
45-125 Panorama Drive
Palm Desert, CA 92260
760-568-9089

Lisa Jackson
LKJ Interiors
8940 Dorrington Ave.
Los Angeles, CA 90048
310-285-9930

Kalman Construction
67 Milestone Road
Nantucket, MA 02554
508-228-5825

Reed Krueger
Reed Krueger & Associates
12 E. Delaware St.
Chicago, IL 60611
312-664-3935

Leslie Jones
Leslie Jones & Associates, Inc.
754 N. Milwaukee Ave.
Chicago, IL 60622
312-455-1147

Raymond Joseph Design
1901 W. Race St.
Chicago, IL 60622
312-733-2312

Erica Lautman Interiors
3100 N. Sheridan Rd.
Chicago, IL 60657
773-665-0051

David MacKenzie
Griskelis + Smith Architects Ltd.
400 N. Michigan Ave., Ste. 500
Chicago, IL 60611
312-645-0011

Kacy and Mark Marcinik
Bottom Duvivier
2603 Broadway
Redwood City, CA 94063
650-361-1209

Brian Murphy
BAM Design
147 W. Channel Rd.
Santa Monica, CA 90404
310-459-0955

Benjamin Noriega-Ortiz
75 Spring St.
New York, NY 10012
212-343-9709

Powell/Kleinschmidt
645 N. Michigan Ave., Ste. 810
Chicago, IL 60611
312-642-6450

Tangee Harris-Pritchett
Tangee Inc.
5306 S. Hyde Park Blvd.
Chicago, IL 60615
773-955-5175

Cindy Simes
Simes Studios
450 W. Surf St.
Chicago, IL 60657
773-327-7101

Kate Stamps
Stamps & Stamps
318 Fairview Lane
South Pasadena, CA 91030

Lenny Steinberg Design
2517 Oceanfront Walk
Venice, CA 90291
310-827-0842

Charles Stewart Architecture
85 Liberty Ship Way, #111
Sausalito, CA 94965
415-331-5339

Tom Stringer
62 W. Huron St.
Chicago, IL 60610
312-664-0644

Jula Sutta
215 Crestview Drive
Orinda, CA 94563
510-253-0862

Lisa Walker
Lisa Walker Design Group Inc.
7125 East 2nd St. Ste. 103
Scottsdale, AZ 85251
480-945-1460

Peter Wheeler
P.J. Wheeler Associates
47 Gray St.
Boston, MA 02116
617-426-5921

Carol Wolk
Carol Wolk Interiors
340 Tudor Ct.
Glencoe, IL 60022
847-835-5500

CATALOGUES AND STORES

Dialogica
484 Broom Street
New York, NY 10013
212-966-1934
or
8304 Melrose Avenue
Los Angeles, CA 90069
323-951-1993

Domain Home Furnishings
51 Morgan Drive
Norwood, MA 02062
617-769-9130

M.J. Foreman
Galleria M
313 W. Superior St.
Chicago, IL 60610
312-988-7790

Ikea
800-434-IKEA for store locations
and ordering information

Richard Kazarian Antiques
11 Church St.
Providence, RI 02904
401-331-0079

Lynette Hand
F. Kia--The Store
558 Tremont St.
Roxbury, MA 02118
617-367-5553

Brad Blair
Lotis Antiquities
158 N. Le Brea Ave.
323-938-4531

Luminaire
301 W. Superior St.
Chicago, IL 60610
800-494-4358
or
2331 Ponce de Leon Blvd.
Coral Gables, FL 33134
800-645-7250

The Morson Collection
100 East Walton St.
Chicago, IL 60611
312-587-7400

Pottery Barn
800-922-5507 for ordering or store information.

Spiegel Catalog
P.O. Box 182555
Columbus, OH 43218
800-345-4500
www.spiegel.com

PHOTOGRAPHERS

Tony Berardi
Photofields
36W830 Stonebridge Lane
St. Charles, IL 60175
630-587-5530

Mark Boisclair
2512 E. Thomas Rd., Ste. 1
Phoenix, AZ 85016
602-957-6997

David Glomb
71340 Estellita Drive
Ranch Mirage, CA 92270
760-340-4455

Kari Haavisto
304 E. 20th Street
New York, NY 10003
212-375-9663

Marco Lorenzetti
Hedrich Blessing
11 W. Illinois St.
Chicago, IL 60610
312-321-1151

Peter Margonelli
20 Desbrosses Street
New York, NY 10013
212-941-0380

Colin McRae
Colin McRae Photography
1061 Folsom Street
San Francisco, CA 94103
415-863-0119
colin@mcraephoto.com

Dorothy Perry
2124 N. Whipple Ave.
Chicago, IL 60647
773-278-5446

Eric Roth
Eric Roth Studio
337 Summer St.
Boston, MA 02210
617-338-5358

Doug Snower Photography
111 W. North Ave.
Chicago, IL 60610
312-943-1500

Tim Street-Porter
2074 Watsonia Terrace
Los Angeles, CA 90068
323-874-4278

ABOUT THE AUTHOR

The Chicago city editor for *Metropolitan Home,* Lisa Skolnik is a regular contributor to the *Chicago Tribune* on design and entertaining, and also writes two nationally syndicated columns for the paper. Her work also has appeared in such publications as *Women's Day, Country Accents,* and *Good HouseKeeping.* Skolnik works in Chicago, where she lives with her husband and four children. She is the author of six books on home design.

DEDICATION

To my children, Caroline, Sasha, Anastasia and Theodora, who all love to loaf, read, nap, and sleep on our progression of gigantic gray sofas, even when they should undoubtedly be in bed. And to Howard, who shares the same obsession, but will forever insist the sofas are brown.

ACKNOWLEDGMENTS

This book would not be possible without a great deal of help and encouragement from many sources.

First, my thanks to Dylan Landis for all her wonderful introductions, including this one to Rockport Publishers.

Further thanks to the staff at Rockport, in particular two remarkable and enterprising women: Shawna Mullen, publisher for Packaged Goods, whose invigorating spirit prompted me to work with Rockport, and Martha Wetherill, acquisitions editor, whose endless enthusiasm and high expectations inspired me to new heights. Both are blessed with gentle, even-tempered and graceful dispositions that made them motivational collaborators. Thanks as well to Francine Hornberger, whose perceptive editing refined, shaped, and arranged the text until it was as flawless as possible. Finally, in a visual book, outstanding graphic design is also critical, so I would like to express my awe and appreciation to Leeann Leftwich and the art department at Rockport Publishers, who made this book far more beautiful than I ever hoped it could be.

I would also like to thank the many photographers, interior designers and architects whose work appears on these pages. Their efforts comprise the core of this book; without their creativity and vision this volume would not be possible. And a special thanks to Sally and Tony Berardi, who turned their files upside down to come up with enough photos to finish this book.

Thank you one and all from the bottom of my heart.